Christmas

Cookies:

Recipes

From Around

the World

Introduction

The Christmas holidays bring family, friends and good cheer. What is Christmas without delicious Christmas cookies? Different cultures around the world all love Christmas cookies but they all have their own variety of this tasty holiday treat. This book is jammed packed with over 80 scrumptious recipes from around the globe. From traditional gingerbread men to the French lace cookies. Enjoy a variety of Christmas cuisines and Merry Christmas, and Happy Holidays to all!

Christmas Sugar Cookies

Ingredients:

1/2 cup butter
1 cup sugar
2 eggs
1 tbsp. milk
2 tsps. baking powder
2 cups flour
1 tsp. vanilla

Directions:

Cream together butter and sugar. Beat in eggs, one at a time, beating after each addition.
Sift flour and baking powder.
Add half of the flour mixture, stir in milk and vanilla, then the remaining flour mixture.
Mix only until combined.
Wrap mixture in plastic wrap and refrigerate for 2 hours or more before rolling out 1/4-inch thick on a lightly floured work surface.
Cut into shapes.
Sprinkle with sugar, cinnamon sugar or grated nuts, if desired.
Bake in a preheated 375 degrees F oven for 10 to 15 minutes or until lightly golden on edges of cookies (depends on size).
Decrease oven temperature if cookies are browning too quickly.

Shortbread Christmas Cookies

Ingredients:

3 cups all-purpose flour
3/4 cup white sugar
1/4 tsp. salt
1 1/2 cups cold butter
1/2 tsp. rum extract
2 tbsps. cold water
2 cups confectioners' sugar
2 tbsps. milk
2 tsps. milk
1 drop food coloring, or to desired shade (optional)
1 tbsp. colored edible glitter, or as desired

Directions:

1. Whisk together flour, sugar, and salt in a large bowl; with a pastry cutter, chop in the butter until the mixture resembles coarse crumbs.
2. Stir the rum extract and almond extract into the water in a small bowl.
3. Mix into the dry ingredients, a little bit at a time, until the mixture holds together in a ball when you squeeze it.
4. Place the dough onto a floured work surface, and sprinkle with flour.
5. Roll out into a sheet 1/4 inch thick. Cut into shapes with floured cookie cutters, and place 1 inch apart on ungreased baking sheets. Cover with a layer of plastic wrap, and refrigerate for 30 minutes.
6. Preheat oven to 325 degrees F (165 degrees C).
7. Bake the cookies just until the edges are lightly browned, 15 to 18 minutes.
8. Allow to cool on sheets for 2 minutes before removing to wire racks to finish cooling.
9. Cool completely before decorating.
10. For frosting, whisk the confectioners' sugar and milk in a bowl until smooth.
11. If desired, divide frosting into small bowls, and tint each bowl a desired shade with food coloring. Frost fully cooled cookies, and sprinkle with edible glitter before the frosting sets.

Chinese Christmas Cookies

Ingredients:

1 cup semisweet chocolate chips
1 cup peanut butter chips
1 cup chow mein noodles
1 cup dry-roasted peanuts

Directions:

1. Melt chocolate and peanut butter chips in the top of a double boiler over simmering water, stirring frequently, until smooth.
2. Mix chow mein noodles and peanuts in a large mixing bowl.
3. Pour chocolate mixture over noodles and peanuts and turn to coat.
4. Line a baking sheet with waxed paper. Drop mixture by rounded tablespoonfuls onto prepared sheet. Refrigerate until set, about 2 hours.

Christmas Casserole Cookies

Ingredients:

2 eggs
1/2 cup white sugar
1 cup chopped dates
1 cup flaked coconut
1 cup chopped walnuts
1 tsp. vanilla extract
1/4 tsp. almond extract

Directions:

1. Preheat oven to 350 degrees F (175 degrees C).
2. In a medium bowl beat eggs with an electric mixer. Beat in sugar.
3. Stir in dates, coconut, walnuts, vanilla and almond extract.
4. Spoon mixture into a 2-quart casserole dish.
5. Bake in preheated oven for 30 minutes.
6. Remove from oven, and while mixture is still hot, beat well with a wooden spoon.
7. When mixture is cool enough to handle, form into small balls and roll in granulated sugar.

Cream Cheese Christmas Cookies

Ingredients:

1 cup butter, softened
1 (8 oz.) package cream cheese
1 cup white sugar
1/2 tsp. vanilla extract
2 1/2 cups all-purpose flour
1/2 tsp. salt
1/2 cup chopped pecans
1/2 cup green sugar crystals
1/2 cup red sugar crystals
1 cup pecan halves

Directions:

1. Cream together the butter and cream cheese.
2. Add sugar and vanilla.
3. Beat until light and fluffy.
4. Combine the flour and salt; gradually add to creamed mixture, beating until well blended.
5. Stir in chopped pecans. Cover bowl with plastic wrap and refrigerate for 15 minutes.
6. On four sheets of aluminum foil, shape dough into four 6 inch rolls, 1 1/2 inches in diameter.
7. Wrap each roll tightly in foil and refrigerate over night.
8. Preheat oven to 325 degrees F (165 degrees C). Line cookie sheets with foil.
9. Remove rolls of dough from refrigerator one at a time. Coat each roll with red or green sugar crystals; cut dough into 1/4 inch slices.
10. Place on prepared cookie sheets; top each cookie with a pecan half. Bake for 15 to 18 minutes or until bottom of cookie is lightly browned when lifted.

Christmas Pumpkin Cookies

Ingredients:

2 cups flour
1 tsp. baking powder
1/2 tsp. baking soda
1 tsp. ground cinnamon
1/2 tsps. salt
1/2 tsp. ground allspice
1/2 tsp. ground ginger
1 cup butter (salted), softened
1 cup sugar
1 cup canned pumpkin
1 large egg
1 tsp. vanilla
1 cup chopped pecans or walnuts
1 cup dried cranberries
1 cup pecan halves

Directions:

1. Preheat oven to 375 degrees F.
2. In a medium mixing bowl, combine flour, baking powder, baking soda, cinnamon, salt, allspice and ginger.
3. In the bowl of an electric mixer at medium speed, cream together butter and sugar until light and fluffy, scraping down sides of bowl once or twice.
4. Add pumpkin, egg and vanilla; beat for 1 minute.
5. Gradually add flour mixture, beating at low speed until well combined.
6. Stir in chopped nuts and cranberries.
7. Drop by large tbsps. onto ungreased baking sheets lined with parchment paper. flatten lightly using the back of a spoon or spatula. Press half of a pecan or walnut into the top of each cookie.
8. Bake 10 to 12 minutes or until golden brown. Remove from oven and let stand for 1 minute before removing with a spatula to a wire rack to cool.
9. Store in an airtight container. May be frozen up to 3 months.

Christmas Cream Cheese Snowball Cookies

Ingredients:

1 cup confectioners' sugar
1/2 cup finely-chopped walnuts
1/2 cup vegetable shortening
1/2 cup butter, softened
1/2 cup cream cheese, softened
1/2 cup white sugar
1/2 tsp. almond extract
1/2 tsp. vanilla extract
1 1/2 cups all-purpose flour

Directions:

1. Preheat oven to 350 degrees F (175 degrees C).
2. Sift the confectioners' sugar into a shallow bowl, stir in the walnuts, and set aside.
3. Beat the shortening, butter, cream cheese, and sugar together in a bowl until the mixture is creamy and thoroughly blended.
4. Mix in the almond extract, vanilla extract, and flour; stir to combine. Scoop up dough by rounded tbsps., and roll into balls about 1 inch in diameter.
5. Place the balls about 1 1/2 inches apart on ungreased baking sheets.
6. Bake in the preheated oven until the cookies turn slightly golden at the edges, about 6 minutes. Let the cookies cool on the baking sheets for about 1 minute, then roll in the confectioners' sugar-walnut mixture while still a little warm.

Christmas Cutout Cookies

Ingredients:

1/3 cup shortening
1 cup sugar
1 egg, beaten
2 tsp. baking powder
1/2 tsp. salt
2 1/2 cup sifted flour
1/2 cup milk
1 tsp. vanilla

Directions:

1. Cream sugar and shortening well, add egg and blend together.
2. Sift together dry ingredients and add to creamed mixture alternately with the milk.
3. Stir in vanilla.
4. Mix, cover and refrigerate for several hours to overnight.
5. Roll out to 1/16 inch thickness on a lightly floured pastry cloth or work surface or between sheets of wax paper.
6. Cut into Christmas designs. Brush with egg white or decorate as desired.
7. Cookies may be decorated before or after baking.
8. Bake at 350 degrees F just until edges are lightly golden, between 10 to 20 minutes.

Cream Cheese Chocolate Chip Cookies

1 (8 oz.) package cream cheese
1 cup margarine
3/4 cup white sugar 3/4 cup packed brown sugar
1 egg
1 tsp. vanilla extract
2 1/2 cups all-purpose flour
1 tsp. baking powder
1/2 tsp. salt
2 cups milk chocolate chips

Directions:

1. Preheat oven to 375 degrees F (190 degrees C).
2. Grease cookie sheets with non-stick butter flavored cooking spray and set aside.
3. Combine cream cheese, margarine, and sugars. Blend in egg and vanilla.
4. Add dry ingredients and mix well. Add chocolate chips and mix.
5. Bake 15-18 minutes or until edges are slightly browned. Enjoy!

Christmas Molasses and Ginger Cookies

Ingredients:

1 1/3 cups molasses
2/3 cup packed brown sugar
2/3 cup butter, softened
5 1/2 cups all-purpose flour
2 eggs
4 tsps. ground cinnamon
2 tsps. baking soda
2 tsps. ground ginger
1 tsp. salt

Directions:

1. Beat molasses, brown sugar, and butter together in a bowl until smooth.
2. Mix flour, eggs, cinnamon, baking soda, ginger, and salt into molasses mixture until incorporated. Cover bowl with plastic wrap and refrigerate for 1 hour.
3. Preheat oven to 375 degrees F (190 degrees C).
4. Line a baking sheet with parchment paper.
5. Heavily flour a cloth-covered work surface.
6. Roll dough on the floured cloth into 1/4-inch thick cookies.
7. Cut with cookie cutters.
8. Arrange cookies 1-inch apart on the prepared baking sheet.
9. Bake in the preheated oven until cookies are firm to the touch, about 8 minutes.
10. Cool in the pans for 10 minutes before removing to cool completely on a wire rack.

Moravian Christmas Ginger Cookies

Ingredients:

3 tbsps. shortening
2 tbsps. brown sugar
1/3 cup molasses
1 1/4 cups all-purpose flour
1/4 tsp. baking soda
1/2 tsp. salt
1/4 tsp. ground cinnamon
1/4 tsp. ground ginger
1/4 tsp. ground cloves
1 pinch ground nutmeg
1 dash ground allspice

Directions:

1. In a medium bowl, cream together the shortening, brown sugar and molasses until smooth.
2. Sift together the flour, baking soda, salt, cinnamon, ginger, cloves, nutmeg and allspice.
3. Blend into the creamed mixture. Work dough with hands until well blended.
4. Cover and chill for about 4 hours. Dough must be thoroughly chilled to hold together.
5. Preheat oven to 375 degrees F (190 degrees C).
6. Roll out dough paper thin a little at a time. Cut into desired shapes using cookie cutters.
7. Place on greased baking sheets.
8. Bake 5 to 6 minutes in the preheated oven, or until lightly browned.

Polish Christmas Cookies

Ingredients:

1 cup butter
1 cup shortening
2 cups white sugar
5 eggs
7 1/2 cups all-purpose flour
6 tsps. baking powder
1/2 tsp. salt
1/2 oz. anise extract

Directions:

1. Preheat oven to 350 degrees F (175 degrees C).
2. Cream the butter, shortening and the sugar together.
3. Stir in the eggs and continue to beat. Add the anise flavoring.
4. Stir in 7 cups of the flour, the baking powder and the salt.
5. Mix until the dough is soft.
6. Add the additional cup of flour if needed.
7. Chill the dough.
8. On a lightly floured surface roll out the dough and cut with cookie cutters.
9. Place cookies on greased cookie sheets.
10. Bake at 350 degrees F (175 degrees C) for 12 to 15 minutes.
11. Frost and decorate when cookies are cooled.

Christmas Cheer Whiskey Cookies

Ingredients:

2 sticks butter, softened
1/2 cup brown sugar
3 eggs
3 cup flour
1 tsp. baking soda
1/2 cup whiskey
1 cup chopped walnuts or slivered almonds
1 cup raisins or dates or glazed fruit

Directions:

1. Cream together butter and sugar; add eggs and beat until mixed.
2. Stir in flour mixed with baking soda.
3. When flour is incorporated, add remaining ingredients.
4. Mix as little as possible to avoid tough cookies.
5. Drop onto parchment sheets and bake in a preheated 350 degrees F degree oven until edges are golden.
6. Remove and cool on wire racks. Store in airtight container.

Pebber Nodder Danish Christmas Cookies

Ingredients:

1 cup butter
1 cup sugar
2 eggs
2 1/2 cups all-purpose flour
1 tsp. ground cardamom
1 tsp. ground cinnamon, or to taste

Directions:

1. Preheat the oven to 350 degrees F (175 degrees C).
2. In a large bowl, mix together the butter and sugar until smooth.
3. Beat in the eggs one at a time, stirring until light and fluffy.
4. Combine the flour, cardamom and cinnamon; stir into the sugar mixture just until blended.
5. Separate the dough into 6 balls, and roll each ball into a rope about as big around as your finger on a lightly floured surface.
6. Cut into 1/2-inch pieces, and place them on an ungreased baking sheet.
7. Bake for 10 minutes in the preheated oven, or until lightly browned.
8. Cool on baking sheets for a few minutes, then transfer to wire racks to cool completely.

Swedish Christmas Cookies (Brunscrackers)

Ingredients:

2 cups flour
1 tsp. baking soda
1 cup butter
1 cup sugar
1 tsp. vanilla sugar
2 tbsps. golden syrup

Directions:

1. Preheat oven to 350 degrees F (175 degrees C). Sift together the flour and baking soda.
2. In a separate bowl, cream together the butter, sugar, vanilla sugar, and golden syrup.
3. Mix well. Stir in the flour and mix until just incorporated.
4. Form dough into two, 1 inch thick elongated rolls the length of your cookie pan. Place them on the cookie pan with enough space in between for them to spread.
5. Bake in preheated oven until they are light golden brown and have flattened; about 20 to 22 minutes if using margarine, or 13 to 15 minutes if using butter.
6. Remove from oven and let cool slightly for about 3 minutes.
7. Cut diagonally into 1 to 2 inch strips while still warm.
8. Remove individual cookies to cool on a wire rack.

Icelandic Christmas Pepper Cookies

All Icelanders bake these cookies for Christmas.

Ingredients:

1 1/4 cups butter, softened
1 1/4 cups white sugar
3/4 cup light corn syrup
2 small eggs
3 cups all-purpose flour
1 1/2 tsps. baking powder
1 tsp. baking soda
1/2 tsp. salt
2 tsps. ground cinnamon
2 tsps. ground cloves
1 tsp. ground ginger
1/4 tsp. ground black pepper

Directions:

1. In a large bowl, cream butter and sugar.
2. Stir in corn syrup and eggs.
3. Cream well.
4. Sift together flour, baking powder, baking soda, salt, cinnamon, cloves, ginger, and pepper.
5. Add dry ingredients to the butter mixture, and mix until smooth.
6. Refrigerate dough over night.
7. Preheat oven to 350 degrees F (175 degrees C).
8. Roll out dough to 1/4 inch thickness.
9. Cut out cookies with a 2 inch round cookie cutter.
10. Place at least 1 inch apart on cookie sheet and bake for 8 to 10 minutes in preheated oven.

Swedish Christmas Spritz Cookies

Ingredients:

3/4 cup blanched slivered almonds
1 cup butter, softened
1 cup sugar
1 egg
1 tsp. almond extract
1 tbsp. milk
2 cups all-purpose flour
1/8 tsp. baking powder
1/4 tsp. salt

Directions:

1. Preheat the oven to 350 degrees F (175 degrees C).
2. Spread the almonds out on a baking sheet.
3. Bake in the preheated oven for 10 to 15 minutes, until lightly browned or until they give off an aroma. Remove from the oven, and allow to cool completely. Grind to a consistency resembling rough sand in a food processor or blender. Be sure almonds are cool, or you will make almond butter.
4. In a medium bowl, cream together the butter and sugar until light and fluffy.
5. Beat in the egg, then stir in the almond extract and milk. Sift in the flour, baking powder and salt, and mix in along with the ground toasted almonds to form a soft dough. Refrigerate the dough for 15 to 20 minutes. This will help the cookies keep their shape after pressing.
6. Lightly grease cookie sheets, and fill cookie press with dough. Press out cookies at least 1 inch apart depending on the size. You can experiment with different cookie designs. I've found most true Swedes tend to use the star shape, however, you're free to use whatever shape suits your fancy.
7. Bake for 8 to 10 minutes in the preheated oven, until cookies are lightly browned.
8. Cool on the cookie sheets for a minute before transferring to a wire rack to cool completely.

Christmas Wise Men Hat Cookies

Ingredients:

1 ¾ cups flour
1 tsp baking soda
1 tsp salt
1/2 cup butter
1/3 cup peanut butter
1/2 cup sugar
1/2 cup brown sugar
1 egg
1 tsp vanilla
1 bag of chocolate candy kisses

Directions:

1. Sift flour, soda and salt.
2. Set aside.
3. Cream butter, peanut butter, and sugar.
4. Add egg & vanilla. Blend in dry ingredients.
5. Shape dough into balls and place on greased cookie sheet.
6. Bake at 375 degrees F for 8 minutes.
7. Do not mash down cookies before baking.
8. When they come out of the oven, immediately put a candy kiss on top of each cookie.
9. When we were little children, we thought the shape these cookies made with the chocolate kisses looked like a hat one of the Three Wise Men might have worn, hence the name of these cookies.

Pebber Nodder (Danish Christmas Cookies)

Ingredients:

1 cup butter
1 cup sugar
2 eggs
2 1/2 cups all-purpose flour
1 tsp. ground cardamom
1 tsp. ground cinnamon, or to taste

Directions:

1. Preheat the oven to 350 degrees F (175 degrees C).
2. In a large bowl, mix together the butter and sugar until smooth.
3. Beat in the eggs one at a time, stirring until light and fluffy.
4. Combine the flour, cardamom and cinnamon; stir into the sugar mixture just until blended.
5. Separate the dough into 6 balls, and roll each ball into a rope about as big around as your finger on a lightly floured surface.
6. Cut into 1/2-inch pieces, and place them on an ungreased baking sheet.
7. Bake for 10 minutes in the preheated oven, or until lightly browned.
8. Cool on baking sheets for a few minutes, then transfer to wire racks to cool completely.

Polish Christmas Cookies

Ingredients:

1 cup butter
1 cup shortening
2 cups white sugar
5 eggs
7 1/2 cups all-purpose flour
6 tsps. baking powder
1/2 tsp. salt
1/2 oz. anise extract

Directions:

1. Preheat oven to 350 degrees F (175 degrees C).
2. Cream the butter, shortening and the sugar together.
3. Stir in the eggs and continue to beat.
4. Add the anise flavoring.
5. Stir in 7 cups of the flour, the baking powder and the salt.
6. Mix until the dough is soft.
7. Add the additional cup of flour if needed.
8. Chill the dough.
9. On a lightly floured surface roll out the dough and cut with cookie cutters.
10. Place cookies on greased cookie sheets.
11. Bake at 350 degrees F (175 degrees C) for 12 to 15 minutes.
12. Frost and decorate when cookies are cooled.

Christmas Fruit Cookies

Ingredients:

1/2 cup butter
1 cup light brown sugar
2 eggs
1 tsp. vanilla
Pinch salt
1 cup unsifted all-purpose flour
2 cup chopped pecans
6 slices candied pineapple, chopped
1/2 lb. candied red cherries

Directions:

1. Preheat oven to 300 degrees F.
2. In large bowl, with electric mixer at high speed, beat butter with sugar until fluffy.
3. Add eggs and beat until light. Add vanilla and salt.
4. At low speed beat in flour until well combined.
5. Grease and flour 9x13x2 inch pan.
6. Drop batter on nuts that have been spread over bottom of greased pan.
7. Press the candied pineapple and cherries into batter.
8. Bake 30 to 40 minutes or until golden.
9. Cut into squares while warm.

Candied Christmas Cookies

Ingredients:

2 eggs
1/2 cup butter, softened
1 cup brown sugar
2 tbsps. orange juice
1 tbsp. bourbon
1 tsp. baking soda
1 tbsp. milk
2 cups all-purpose flour
3 cups candied cherries
3 cups dates, pitted and chopped
4 cups chopped pecans

Directions:

1. Preheat oven to 350 degrees F.
2. Grease cookie sheets.
3. In large mixing bowl, cream together eggs, butter and brown sugar.
4. Mix baking soda with the milk and add to mixture.
5. Stir in orange juice and bourbon.
6. In a small bowl, lightly toss candied fruits with a small amount of flour until fruits separate easily.
7. Add to mixture. Add flour, dates and pecans.
8. Stir until well blended.
9. Drop by tsps. about 2 inches apart onto cookie sheet.
10. Bake for 8 to 10 minutes in the preheated oven.
11. Allow cookies to cool on baking sheet for 5 minutes before removing to a wire rack to cool completely.

Bon Bon Christmas Cookies

Ingredients:

1/2 (8 oz.) package cream cheese
1/2 cup butter flavored shortening
2 cups sifted all-purpose flour
1 1/2 cups sifted confectioners' sugar
2 (10 oz.) jars maraschino cherries, drained

Directions:

1. In a medium bowl, stir together the shortening and cream cheese until well blended.
2. Stir in the flour, you may need to use your hands to help it form a dough.
3. If the mixture seems too dry, add a couple of tsps. of water.
4. Cover and chill several hours or overnight.
5. Preheat the oven to 375 degrees F (190 degrees C).
6. Lightly grease cookie sheets.
7. Before rolling out the dough, dust the rolling surface heavily with confectioners' sugar.
8. Roll the dough out to 1/8 inch thickness.
9. Cut into 1x4 inch strips.
10. Place a cherry on the end of each strip.
11. Roll up each strip starting with the cherry.
12. Place on prepared cookie sheets and dust with a little of the confectioners' sugar.
13. Bake for 7 to 10 minutes in the preheated oven.
14. Cookies should brown slightly.
15. Dust again with the confectioners' sugar.
16. Allow cookies to cool before serving, the cherries are very hot!

Christmas Lizzies

Ingredients:

1/4 cup butter
1/2 cup packed brown sugar
2 eggs
1 1/2 cups all-purpose flour
1 1/2 tsps. baking soda
1 1/2 tsps. ground cinnamon
1 1/2 tsps. ground nutmeg
1/2 tsp. ground cloves
3 cups raisins
1/2 cup bourbon
4 cups pecan halves
3 cups candied cherries
1/3 pound diced candied lemon peel

Directions:

1. Soak fruits in bourbon at least 1 hour to plump.
2. Preheat oven to 325 degrees F (170 degrees C).
3. Grease cookie sheets.
4. Cream margarine or butter, gradually adding sugar and eggs.
5. Add dry ingredients, then fruit and nuts. Mix well.
6. Drop from tsp. onto greased cookie sheets. Bake for 15 minutes.
7. Store in an airtight container.

Christmas Raisin Delights

Ingredients:

3 1/2 cups all-purpose flour
2 tsps. baking powder
1 tsp. salt
2/3 cup butter, softened
3/4 cup packed brown sugar
3/4 cup white sugar
2 eggs
1/3 cup milk
1 tsp. vanilla
1 3/4 cups raisins
1 cup packed brown sugar
1 cup water
1 pinch salt
1 tsp. lemon juice
1 1/2 tbsps. cornstarch
2 tbsps. water
1/2 cup chopped walnuts

Dough Directions:

1. Sift the flour, baking powder, and salt together.
2. set aside.
3. Cream the butter with 3/4 cup of the brown sugar and the white sugar.
4. Beat in the eggs, milk and vanilla.
5. Mix at high speed for 2 minutes, then reduce speed and gradually blend in the flour mixture. Cover and refrigerate dough for at least 3 hours.
6. Grind the raisins.
7. In a medium saucepan combine the ground raisins, 1 cup brown sugar, 1 cup water, salt and lemon juice. Bring to a boil, and simmer for 3 minutes.
8. Combine the cornstarch and 2 tbsps. of the water and mix until smooth. Add to the raisin mixture and continue to simmer until thick. Remove from heat and let cool. Once cool, stir in the chopped nuts.
9. Preheat Oven to 350 degrees F (175 degrees C). Lightly grease baking sheets.
10. On a floured surface, roll out the chilled dough to 1/8 inch thick.
11. Cut into 2 3/4 inch rounds.

12. Place rounds on the prepared baking sheet. Place a heaping tsp. of the raisin filling on the cookie round and top with another round. Crimp the edges closed.
13. Bake at 350 degrees F (175 degrees C) for 8 minutes.
14. Allow cookies to cool on sheet until just barely warm.

Christmas Cornflake Wreath Cookie

Ingredients:

1/2 cup butter
4 cups miniature marshmallows
1 tsp. green food coloring
1/2 tsp. almond extract
1/2 tsp. vanilla extract 4 cups cornflakes cereal
1 (2.25 oz.) package cinnamon red hot candies

Directions:

1. Microwave marshmallows and butter on High for 2 minutes.
2. Stir, then microwave on High for 2 minutes more.
3. Stir.
4. Add and mix quickly the coloring, extracts, then cornflakes.
5. Drop by spoonfuls in clumps on greased wax paper and decorate with 3 red hots each.
6. Once cool, transfer to lightly greased serving/storage tray with lightly greased fingers.

Scandinavian Peppernotter Christmas Cookies

Ingredients:

3 eggs
3/4 cup white sugar
3/4 cup brown sugar
2 tsps. lemon juice
2/3 cup finely chopped almonds (optional)
1 tsp. baking powder
1 tsp. ground cinnamon
1 tsp. ground ginger
1 tsp. ground black pepper
1/2 tsp. ground allspice
1/2 tsp. ground cloves
3 cups all-purpose flour
1 cup confectioners' sugar
2 tsps. water

Directions:

1. Preheat oven to 300 degrees F (150 degrees C).
2. Grease several baking sheets.
3. Beat the eggs, white sugar, and brown sugar in a bowl until the sugar has dissolved, then beat in lemon juice, almonds, baking powder, cinnamon, ginger, black pepper, allspice, and cloves until thoroughly combined.
4. Mix in flour to make a sticky dough.
5. Turn the dough out onto a well-floured work surface, and knead the dough 1 to 2 minutes, adding more flour if needed, to make a smooth, workable dough.
6. Pinch off pieces of dough and roll them into balls about 1 1/2 inches in diameter, and place the balls on the prepared baking sheets at least 1 inch apart.
7. Bake in the preheated oven until a toothpick inserted into the center of a cookie comes out clean, about 25 minutes.
8. Remove from sheets immediately to cooling racks to prevent cookies from getting too hard.
9. Stir together confectioners' sugar and water to make a glaze, and drizzle each cookie while slightly warm with about 1/2 tsp., spreading it around the top of the cookie.

Polish Christmas Cookies

Ingredients:

1 cup butter
1 cup shortening
2 cups white sugar
5 eggs
7 1/2 cups all-purpose flour
6 tsps. baking powder
1/2 tsp. salt
1/2 oz. anise extract

Directions:

1. Preheat oven to 350 degrees F (175 degrees C).
2. Cream the butter, shortening and the sugar together.
3. Stir in the eggs and continue to beat. Add the anise flavoring.
4. Stir in 7 cups of the flour, the baking powder and the salt.
5. Mix until the dough is soft.
6. Add the additional cup of flour if needed.
7. Chill the dough.
8. On a lightly floured surface roll out the dough and cut with cookie cutters. Place cookies on greased cookie sheets.
9. Bake at 350 degrees F (175 degrees C) for 12 to 15 minutes.
10. Frost and decorate when cookies are cooled.

Italian Christmas Cookie

Ingredients:

3 1/2 cups all-purpose flour, or as needed
4 tsps. baking powder
1 cup white sugar
1/2 cup butter, softened
4 eggs 1 cup cocoa powder
2 tbsps. orange-flavored liqueur
2 tsps. vanilla extract

Icing Ingredients:

2 cups sifted confectioners' sugar
2 tbsps. orange-flavored liqueur
2 tbsps. water
2 tsps. vanilla extract

Directions:

1. Preheat oven to 375 degrees F (190 degrees C).
2. Grease 2 baking sheets.
3. Sift flour and baking powder together in a bowl.
4. Beat white sugar and butter together in a separate bowl using an electric mixer until smooth and creamy; beat in eggs.
5. Stir creamed butter mixture, cocoa powder, 2 tbsps. liqueur, and 2 tsps. vanilla extract into flour mixture until dough is just combined.
6. Turn dough onto a lightly floured work surface and knead, adding flour as needed to keep from dough sticking to your hands.
7. Roll dough, 1 to 2 tbsps. per cookie, in your hands and form a log-shape; twirl log into desired shape.
8. Place cookies on the prepared baking sheet.
9. Bake in the preheated oven until edges of cookies are lightly browned, about 10 minutes.
10. Stir confectioners' sugar, 2 tbsps. liqueur, water, and 2 tsps. vanilla extract together in a bowl until icing is creamy.
11. Dip cookies into icing. Place a piece of waxed paper under a wire rack and place cookies on wire rack to cool.

Italian Butterball Christmas Cookies

Ingredients:

1 stick butter
3/4 cup confectioners' sugar
1 egg
1 tsp. vanilla extract
1 tsp. almond extract
1 1/2 cups all-purpose flour
2 tsps. baking powder
1 pinch salt
1/4 cup confectioners' sugar

Directions:

1. Preheat an oven to 350 degrees F (175 degrees C).
2. Grease a baking sheet.
3. Beat together the butter and 3/4 cup confectioners' sugar with an electric mixer in a large bowl until smooth.
4. Add the egg, vanilla extract, and almond extract.
5. Stir together the flour, baking powder, and salt in a bowl and mix into the butter mixture until just incorporated.
6. Shape the dough into 1-inch balls and arrange on the prepared baking sheet spaced about 2 inches apart.
7. Bake in the preheated oven until firm, about 10 minutes.
8. Cool on the sheet for 10 minutes before removing to cool completely on a wire rack.
9. Spread the 1/4 cup confectioners sugar on a plate.
10. Roll the cooled cookies in the confectioners' sugar to coat.

Italian Chocolate Christmas Cookies

Ingredients:

3 cups all-purpose flour
4 tsps. baking powder
3/4 cup white sugar
1/4 cup unsweetened cocoa powder
1 cup butter, softened
1/3 cup milk
1 tsp. vanilla extract
1/2 cup chopped walnuts
2 (1 oz.) squares unsweetened chocolate
1 tbsp. butter, softened
1 tsp. vanilla extract
2 cups confectioners' sugar
1/4 cup hot milk

Directions:

1. Preheat oven to 375 degrees F (190 degrees C).
2. Sift 3 cups flour twice. In a large bowl, mix flour, baking powder, white sugar and cocoa. Cream 1 cup butter or margarine.
3. Blend into flour mixture. Add 1/3 cup milk, 1 tsp. vanilla and nuts.
4. Mix thoroughly with hands until well blended.
5. Dough should be the consistency of pie crust, but not sticky.
6. For each cookie, pinch off about 1 tsp. dough.
7. Roll by hands into balls, each about one-inch in diameter.
8. Place on greased baking sheets. Do not flatten. Bake about 10 minutes, until lightly browned. Remove from baking sheets; cool on racks. When cool, drizzle each generously with chocolate frosting. Sprinkle with candy sprinkles if desired.

Frosting Directions:

1. Melt the chocolate squares over low heat.
2. Cream with 1 tbsp. of butter or margarine, 1 tsp. vanilla and 2 cups of confectioner's sugar.
3. Gradually add hot milk, beating until smooth.

Italian Christmas Champagne Cookies

Ingredients:

1/2 cup multicolored candy sprinkles
1/2 cup shortening
1 cup white sugar
1 cup champagne
2 cups all-purpose flour
2 tsps. baking powder
4 drops red food coloring

Directions:

1. Preheat oven to 375 degrees F (190 degrees C).
2. Place the sprinkles in a shallow bowl.
3. Beat the shortening and sugar in a bowl with an electric mixer until the mixture is light and creamy.
4. Pour in the champagne, and mix for about 1 minute on low speed.
5. Mixture will be lumpy.
6. Mix in the baking powder, and stir in flour to make a smooth dough.
7. Stir in red food coloring by drops until the mixture is desired shade of pink.
8. Pinch off about 1 rounded tbsp. of dough, roll into a ball, and dip the ball into the sprinkles, covering the top.
9. Place the ball onto a baking sheet with the sprinkles up, and repeat with the rest of the dough. Use the bottom of a glass to press the cookies flat.
10. Bake in the preheated oven until the edges of the cookies are very lightly browned and the cookies are crisp, 12 to 14 minutes.
11. Let cool 1 minute on baking sheet before removing to a rack to finish cooling.

Lemon Christmas Cookies

Ingredients:

1/3 cup white sugar
1 egg
2/3 cup honey
1 tsp. lemon extract
2 3/4 cups sifted all-purpose flour
1 tsp. baking soda
1 tsp. salt

Directions:

1. Mix sugar, egg, honey, and lemon in a medium bowl with mixer.
2. Sift together and stir in flour, soda, and salt.
3. Chill dough for 1 hour.
4. Preheat oven to 375 degrees F (190 degrees C).
5. Roll out 1/4 inch dough and cut shapes using flour to roll and cut.
6. Place on greased cookie sheets. Bake for 8-10 minutes.
7. Do not let cookies get brown.
8. Follow by icing with a butter cream icing.

Peanut Butter Christmas Mice Cookies

Ingredients:

1/2 cup butter, room temperature
1 cup creamy peanut butter
1/2 cup packed light brown sugar
1/2 cup white sugar
1 egg 1 tsp. vanilla extract
1/2 tsp. baking soda
1 1/2 cups all-purpose flour
1 cup peanut halves
1/4 cup green candy sprinkles
60 3-inch pieces red shoestring licorice

Directions:

1. In a large bowl combine butter and peanut butter.
2. Beat until creamy.
3. Add brown and white sugar and beat until fluffy.
4. Beat in egg, vanilla extract and baking soda until well blended.
5. With mixer on low, mix in flour just until blended.
6. Cover and chill for 1 hour, or until firm.
7. Preheat oven to 350 degrees F (175 degrees C).
8. Shape 1 level tbsp. of dough into 1 inch balls.
9. Taper each ball at one end into a teardrop shape. Press flat on one side. Place flat sides down, 2 inches apart on ungreased cookie sheets.
10. Press the sides of the dough in to raise the 'backs' of the mice, as dough will spread slightly during baking.
11. Gently push 2 peanut halves in each 'mouse' for ears, and 2 pieces of green candy for eyes. With a toothpick make a hole 1/2 inch deep in the tail ends.
12. Bake in preheated oven for 8 to 10 minutes, or until firm.
13. Transfer to a cooling rack and insert licorice pieces as tails.

Christmas Lizzies

Ingredients:

1/4 cup butter
1/2 cup packed brown sugar
2 eggs
1 1/2 cups all-purpose flour
1 1/2 tsps. baking soda
1 1/2 tsps. ground cinnamon
1 1/2 tsps. ground nutmeg
1/2 tsp. ground cloves
3 cups raisins
1/2 cup bourbon
4 cups pecan halves
3 cups candied cherries
1/3 pound diced candied lemon peel

Directions:

1. Soak fruits in bourbon at least 1 hour to plump.
2. Preheat oven to 325 degrees F (170 degrees C).
3. Grease cookie sheets.
4. Cream margarine or butter, gradually adding sugar and eggs.
5. Add dry ingredients, then fruit and nuts. Mix well.
6. Drop from tsp. onto greased cookie sheets. Bake for 15 minutes.
7. Store in an airtight container.

Christmas Orange Balls

Ingredients:

4 cups graham cracker crumbs
1 cup confectioners' sugar
1 (6 oz.) can frozen orange juice concentrate, thawed
1 cup chopped pecans
1/4 cup light corn syrup
1/4 cup butter, melted
1/3 cup confectioners' sugar for decoration

Directions:

1. In a medium bowl, stir together the graham cracker crumbs, confectioners' sugar and pecans.
2. Make a well in the center and pour in the orange juice concentrate, corn syrup and melted butter.
3. Mix well by hand until dough forms.
4. Roll into 1 inch balls and roll the balls in confectioners' sugar.
5. Store at room temperature in an airtight container.
6. Put a sheet of waxed paper between layers to prevent sticking.

Christmas Cherry Rum Balls

Ingredients:

1/2 cup rum
1/4 cup light corn syrup
3 cups vanilla wafer crumbs
1 1/2 cups chopped pecans
1 cup confectioners' sugar
24 red candied cherries, halved

Directions:

1. Melt the chocolate chips and stir in the rum and corn syrup.
2. Stir together the vanilla wafer crumbs, pecans and 1/2 cup of the confectioners' sugar.
3. Drizzle the chocolate mixture over the crumb mixture and stir until blended.
4. Shape mixture into 1 inch balls.
5. Roll balls in the remaining confectioners' sugar.
6. Place cherry half in center of each cookie, pressing down lightly.
7. Store in an airtight container for several days to develop flavor.

Mexican Christmas Wedding Cookies

Ingredients:

1 cup butter, softened
8 tbsps. confectioners' sugar
2 cups all-purpose flour
2 cups chopped walnuts
1/2 tsp. vanilla extract

Directions:

1. Preheat oven to 350 degrees F (180 degrees C).
2. Mix all the ingredients together with a mixer until well blended.
3. Roll dough into round small balls.
4. Bake for 10-12 minutes.
5. Cool completely then roll in additional confectionary sugar.

Irish Christmas Soda Bread Cookies

Ingredients:

2 cups all-purpose flour
3/4 cup white sugar
1/2 tsp. baking soda
1/2 cup butter
1/2 cup dried currants
1/4 cup buttermilk
1 egg
1/4 tsp. salt
1 tsp. caraway seed

Directions:

1. Preheat oven to 350 degrees F (175 degrees C).
2. Combine dry ingredients in a mixing bowl.
3. With a pastry blender, cut in butter until mixture resembles coarse meal. Stir in currants.
4. Mix in beaten egg. Pour in milk and mix with a fork to make a soft dough (may need a little more milk).
5. On a floured surface, shape dough into a ball and knead lightly 5 or 6 times. Roll out dough to 1/4 inch thick and cut into squares and triangles with a knife (approximately 2 inches in diameter).
6. Bake for 12 to 14 minutes or until slightly browned.

Irish Christmas Cream Sugar Cookies

Ingredients:

1 cup butter, softened
1 1/2 cups white sugar
1 tsp. vanilla extract
1 egg yolk
1 egg
1/2 cup Irish cream liqueur
4 cups all-purpose flour
1/2 tsp. salt
1 tbsp. baking powder

Directions:

1. Cream together butter and sugar until fluffy.
2. Beat in vanilla and egg yolk until combined, then beat in egg; beat until smooth. Pour in Irish cream, and beat until incorporated.
3. Sift together flour, salt, and baking powder.
4. Stir into butter mixture until evenly mixed. Form into a flattened ball, wrap well with plastic wrap, and refrigerate 2 hours to overnight.
5. Preheat oven to 350 degrees F (175 degrees C).
6. Line two baking sheets with parchment paper.
7. Roll dough out to 1/4 inch thickness on a floured work surface.
8. Cut into shapes using cookie cutters and place onto prepared baking sheets.
9. Bake in preheated oven until golden brown around the edges, 6 to 8 minutes.
10. Cool on a wire rack until they reach room temperature.

Irish Christmas Shamrock Cookies

Ingredients:

1/2 cup butter, softened
1 (3 oz.) package instant pistachio pudding mix
1 1/3 cups baking mix
1 egg
1 tbsp. white sugar

Directions:

1. Preheat oven to 350 degrees F (175 degrees C).
2. Lightly grease baking sheet.
3. Cream together the butter or margarine and the pudding mix.
4. Blend in the baking mix, egg and sugar and mix well.
5. On a lightly floured surface roll out the dough to 3/8 inch thickness and cut into cookies with a shamrock cookie cutter.
6. Place cookies on the prepared baking sheet and bake at 350 degrees F (175 degrees C) for 9 to 10 minutes or until lightly browned on the edges.
7. Let cookies cool on rack.
8. Frost with green colored icing if desired.

Irish Christmas Flag Cookies

Ingredients:

1 cup butter
1 1/2 cups confectioners' sugar
1 egg
1 tsp. vanilla extract
2 1/2 cups all-purpose flour
1 tsp. baking soda
1 tsp. cream of tartar

Directions:

1. In a large bowl, cream together butter and confectioners' sugar.
2. Beat in egg and vanilla extract.
3. Mix well.
4. In a medium sized bowl, stir together the flour, baking soda and cream of tartar. Blend into the butter mixture.
5. Divide dough into thirds and shape into balls.
6. Working with 1/3 of the dough at a time, roll out dough to 1/4 inch thick on a floured surface. With a knife, cut dough into rectangles about 2 inches high by 3 inches long. (6 x 8 cm).
7. Place rectangles on an ungreased cookie sheet, 2 inches apart.
8. Bake in a preheated 350 degree F (175 degrees C) oven until lightly browned.
9. Cool completely on wire rack.

Irish Christmas Oatmeal Cookies

Ingredients:

1 1/4 cups coconut oil
1/2 cup firmly packed brown sugar
1/2 cup white sugar
1 egg 1 tsp. vanilla extract
1 1/2 cups whole wheat flour
1 tsp. baking soda
1 tsp. coarse salt
3 cups quick-cooking Irish oatmeal
1 egg, beaten (optional)
1/2 cup golden raisins
1/2 cup chopped almonds

Directions:

1. Preheat oven to 350 degrees F (175 degrees C).
2. Grease 18 muffin cups with coconut oil.
3. Beat coconut oil, brown sugar, and white sugar with an electric mixer in a large bowl until smooth. Mix in the flour mixture until just incorporated.
4. Beat 1 egg and vanilla extract into the coconut oil mixture.
5. Whisk flour, baking soda, and coarse salt together in a bowl.
6. Beat into the coconut oil mixture until a dough forms.
7. Fold oatmeal, raisins, and almonds into dough.
8. Mix beaten egg into dough if needed for moisture.
9. Spoon dough into prepared muffin cups to about half full.
10. Bake in preheated oven until center is set and top is lightly browned, 12 to 14 minutes.

Welsh Christmas Cookies

Ingredients:

2 cups all-purpose flour
2 tsps. baking powder
1 pinch salt
1/2 cup white sugar
1/4 cup butter
1/4 cup shortening
1/2 cup dried currants
1 egg
1/4 cup milk
1/3 cup granulated sugar for decoration

Directions:

1. Mix flour, baking powder, salt and the 1/2 cup sugar in medium bowl until well blended.
2. Cut in butter or margarine and shortening with a pastry blender until mixture is crumbly.
3. Toss in currants.
4. Beat egg and milk with a fork in a 1-cup measure.
5. Add to flour mixture; mix gently with fork, just until blended.
6. Dough should be consistency of pastry dough.
7. Roll out dough to 1/4 inch thickness with floured rolling pin on lightly floured pastry cloth or board.
8. Cut with 3 inch floured cookie cutter
9. Heat greased griddle or large heavy skillet over moderate heat until few drops of water jump when dropped on surface.
10. Cook cakes, a few at a time, 3 minutes, or until golden brown.
11. Turn with pancake turner and cook another 3 minutes, or until golden brown on second side.
12. Remove to wire rack. Sprinkle with sugar.
13. Let cool completely, then wrap in plastic bags to store.

Canadian Christmas Molasses Cookies

Ingredients:

1 cup dark molasses
3/4 cup packed brown sugar
1 tsp. cider vinegar
2 1/3 cups all-purpose flour
1 1/2 tsps. ground ginger
2 tsps. baking soda
1 egg
1/2 tsp. salt

Directions:

1. Preheat oven to 350 degrees F (175 degrees C).
2. Grease cookie sheets.
3. In a large bowl, stir together the molasses, brown sugar, vinegar, and egg. Sift together the flour, baking soda, ginger and salt; add to molasses mixture. Mix until well blended. Spoon the dough by teaspoonfuls onto cookie sheets, about 2 inches apart.
4. Bake until edges are golden, 12 to 15 minutes. Let cool on pans for 5 minutes before removing.

Eskimo Christmas Cookies

Ingredients:

3/4 cup butter
3/4 cup white sugar
3 tbsps. unsweetened cocoa powder
1/2 tsp. vanilla extract
1 tbsp. water
2 cups rolled oats
1/3 cup confectioners' sugar for decoration

Directions:

1. Soften butter and beat well.
2. Add sugar and mix well.
3. Add cocoa, vanilla and water.
4. Then add oatmeal.
5. Shape into 36 balls and roll in confectioners' sugar.
6. Store in refrigerator.

French Christmas Peppermint Cookies

Ingredients:

3 egg whites at room temperature
1/4 cup white sugar
1/4 tsp. cream of tartar
1 dash peppermint extract, or to taste
2 cups confectioners' sugar, or as needed
1 (6 oz.) package semisweet chocolate chips
3/4 cup heavy whipping cream, or as needed
1 tsp. white sugar, or to taste
1 peppermint candy cane, finely crushed

Directions:

1. Move rack to the bottom of oven and preheat oven to 175 degrees F (80 degrees C).
2. Line baking sheets with aluminum foil.
3. Whisk egg whites and 1/4 cup white sugar in the top of a double boiler set over simmering water until smooth. Whisk cream of tartar and peppermint extract into egg mixture and beat until foamy.
4. Gradually whisk confectioners' sugar into mixture, beating until egg white meringue holds stiff peaks.
5. Scoop about 1 tbsp. of meringue per cookie and gently transfer to the prepared baking sheets; use spoon to shape the meringue cookies into football shape with 2 gently pointed ends.
6. Bake cookies on bottom rack of the preheated oven until dry on the outside but still slightly soft in the centers, about 1 1/2 hours. Let cool completely before removing from baking sheets.
7. Melt chocolate chips in the top of a double boiler over simmering water until melted, stirring until smooth.
8. Gradually mix cream into chocolate until mixture is thick but not pasty.
9. Stir 1 tsp. white sugar into chocolate ganache until sugar has dissolved.
10. Dip cookies in ganache.
11. Place dipped cookies atop a piece of parchment paper and sprinkle with crushed peppermint candy.
12. Let cookies set; refrigerate leftovers.

French Christmas Lace Cookies

Ingredients:

1/2 cup light corn syrup
1/2 cup shortening
2/3 cup packed brown sugar
1 cup all-purpose flour
1 cup chopped pecans

Directions:

1. Preheat oven to 350 degrees F (175 degrees C).
2. Prepare cookie sheets by covering with parchment.
3. In a medium saucepan, heat the corn syrup, shortening and brown sugar over medium heat.
4. Stir constantly until the mixture comes to a boil.
5. In a small bowl toss together the flour and nuts; stir into the saucepan mixture, and remove from the heat.
6. Keep the batter warm by setting over a pan of hot water.
7. Drop by teaspoonfuls onto the prepared cookie sheets.
8. Cookies should be at least 3 inches apart.
9. Bake for about 5 minutes, until the center of the cookie is set.
10. Let the cookies set before removing from the baking sheets.

French Christmas Madeleines

Ingredients:

2 eggs
3/4 tsp. vanilla extract
1/8 tsp. salt
1/3 cup white sugar
1/2 cup all-purpose flour
1 tbsp. lemon zest
1/4 cup butter
1/3 cup granulated sugar for decoration

Directions:

1. Preheat oven to 375 degrees F (190 degrees C).
2. Butter and flour 12 (3 inch) madeleine molds.
3. Set aside.
4. Melt butter and let cool to room temperature.
5. In a small mixing bowl, beat eggs, vanilla and salt at high speed until light.
6. Beating constantly, gradually add sugar; and continue beating at high speed until mixture is thick and pale and ribbons form in bowl when beaters are lifted, 5 to 10 minutes.
7. Sift flour into egg mixture 1/3 at a time, gently folding after each addition.
8. Add lemon zest and pour melted butter around edge of batter.
9. Quickly but gently fold butter into batter. Spoon batter into molds; it will mound slightly above tops.
10. Bake 14 to 17 minutes, or until cakes are golden and the tops spring back when gently pressed with your fingertip.
11. Use the tip of the knife to loosen madeleines from pan and invert onto rack. Sprinkle cookies with granulated sugar.

French Christmas Crullers

Ingredients:

4 tbsps. white sugar
1 tsp. salt
1 tsp. orange zest
4 tbsps. shortening
1 cup hot water
1 cup all-purpose flour
3 eggs
1 1/2 tbsps. shortening
1 1/2 cups confectioners' sugar
3 tbsps. cream
1/8 tsp. salt
1 tsp. vanilla extract

Directions:

1. Put 4 tbsps. sugar, salt, shortening and orange rind in saucepan with 1 cup hot water.
2. Bring to a boil.
3. Mix in 1 cup of flour.
4. Cook until thick, stirring constantly. Remove from heat, and cool slightly. Beat in one egg at a time, beating each one in thoroughly before adding another.
5. Using a rose tip, press dough through pastry bag, in desired shape, onto a well-greased square of heavy paper. Turn paper upside down and let crullers drop into deep, hot fat (375 degrees F - 190 degrees C).
6. Fry until well puffed up and golden brown in color, about 6 to 7 minutes. Drain on unglazed paper.
7. Ice with confectioners' frosting.

Frosting Directions:

1. Cream 1 1/2 tbsps. shortening and continue creaming while slowly adding sugar.
2. Add cream, salt, and vanilla and mix smooth.

French Christmas Macaroons

Ingredients:

3 egg whites
1/4 cup white sugar
1 2/3 cups confectioners' sugar
1 cup finely ground almonds

Directions:

1. Line a baking sheet with a silicone baking mat.
2. Beat egg whites in the bowl of a stand mixer fitted with a whisk attachment until whites are foamy; beat in white sugar and continue beating until egg whites are glossy, fluffy, and hold soft peaks.
3. Sift confectioners' sugar and ground almonds in a separate bowl and quickly fold the almond mixture into the egg whites, about 30 strokes.
4. Spoon a small amount of batter into a plastic bag with a small corner cut off and pipe a test disk of batter, about 1 1/2 inches in diameter, onto prepared baking sheet. If the disk of batter holds a peak instead of flattening immediately, gently fold the batter a few more times and retest.
5. When batter is mixed enough to flatten immediately into an even disk, spoon into a pastry bag fitted with a plain round tip.
6. Pipe the batter onto the baking sheet in rounds, leaving space between the disks. Let the piped cookies stand out at room temperature until they form a hard skin on top, about 1 hour.
7. Preheat oven to 285 degrees F (140 degrees C).
8. Bake cookies until set but not browned, about 10 minutes; let cookies cool completely before filling.

French Christmas Peppermint Meringues

Ingredients:

2 egg whites
1/8 tsp. salt
1/8 tsp. cream of tartar
1/2 cup white sugar
2 peppermint candy canes, crushed

Directions:

1. Preheat oven to 225 degrees F (110 degrees C).
2. Line 2 cookie sheets with foil.
3. In a large glass or metal mixing bowl, beat egg whites, salt, and cream of tartar to soft peaks.
4. Gradually add sugar, continuing to beat until whites form stiff peaks.
5. Drop by spoonfuls 1 inch apart on the prepared cookie sheets.
6. Sprinkle crushed peppermint candy over the cookies.
7. Bake for 1 1/2 hours in preheated oven. Meringues should be completely dry on the inside. Do not allow them to brown. Turn off oven.
8. Keep oven door ajar, and let meringues sit in the oven until completely cool. Loosen from foil with metal spatula.
9. Store loosely covered in cool dry place for up to 2 months.

Christmas Peppermint Snowballs

Ingredients:

3 cups confectioners' sugar
1 1/4 cups butter, softened
1 tsp. peppermint extract
1 tsp. vanilla extract
1 egg
3 cups all-purpose flour
1 tsp. baking powder
1/2 tsp. salt
1 cup white sugar, or as needed
1 cup finely crushed peppermint candy

Directions:

1. Preheat oven to 350 degrees F (175 degrees C).
2. Lightly grease baking sheets, or line with parchment paper.
3. Beat 1 1/2 cups confectioners' sugar with the butter, peppermint extract, vanilla extract, and egg in a mixing bowl at Medium speed until well blended and creamy, 2 to 3 minutes. Reduce speed to Low, and gradually mix in the flour, baking powder, and salt until well blended, 1 to 2 minutes. Stir in 1/2 cup crushed peppermint candy using a wooden spoon.
4. Place the white sugar in a shallow bowl.
5. Roll a small amount of cookie dough between your hands to make 3/4 inch diameter balls. Roll in sugar. Place 1 inch apart on prepared baking sheets.
6. Bake in preheated oven until light brown, 10 to 12 minutes.
7. Remove and cool on racks.
8. Meanwhile, to make the glaze, stir the remaining 1 1/2 cups confectioners sugar together with the milk in a bowl until smooth.
9. Drizzle cooled cookies with the glaze, and sprinkle immediately with the remaining crushed peppermint candy.

Peppermint Holiday Cookies

Ingredients:

1 cup butter, softened
3/4 cup white sugar
1 egg, beaten
3 cups all-purpose flour
1/4 tsp. salt
1/2 cup crushed peppermint candy canes
3/4 cup confectioners' sugar
5 tsps. warm water
2 tbsps. crushed peppermint candy canes

Directions:

1. Preheat oven to 350 degrees F (175 degrees C).
2. Beat the butter and white sugar with an electric mixer in a large bowl until smooth. Beat egg into butter mixture until completely incorporated.
3. Mix flour and salt into the butter mixture until just incorporated.
4. Fold crushed candy canes into the batter, mixing just enough to evenly combine. Roll dough into balls 1 tbsp. at a time; arrange on baking sheets.
5. Bake in the preheated oven until firm, 8 to 10 minutes.
6. Allow cookies to cool on the baking sheet for 1 minute before removing to a wire rack to cool completely.
7. Whisk confectioners' sugar and warm water together in a small bowl until you have a smooth icing.
8. Dip top of each cookie in the icing.
9. Top with additional crushed candy cane, if desired.
10. Set aside to let the icing dry, at least 5 minutes.

Christmas Chocolate Chip Peppermint Cookies

Ingredients:

3/4 cup butter
1/2 cup white sugar
1/2 cup packed brown sugar
1 egg
1 tsp. vanilla extract
1 tsp. peppermint extract
1 1/2 cups all-purpose flour
1/4 cup unsweetened cocoa powder
1 tsp. baking soda
1/4 tsp. salt
1 cup semisweet chocolate chips

Directions:

1. Preheat oven to 350 degrees F (175 degrees C).
2. Grease cookie sheets.
3. In a large bowl, cream together butter, white sugar, and brown sugar until light and fluffy.
4. Beat in egg, then stir in vanilla and peppermint extracts. Combine flour, cocoa powder, baking soda, and salt.
5. Gradually stir into the creamed mixture. Mix in the chocolate chips.
6. Drop by rounded spoonfuls onto the prepared cookie sheets.
7. Bake for 12 to 15 minutes in the preheated oven.
8. Allow cookies to cool on cookie sheets for 5 minutes before transferring to a wire rack to cool completely.

German Holiday Spice Cookies (Lebkuchen)

Ingredients:

2 cups whole almonds boiling water to cover
2/3 cup chopped dried apricots
8 Medjool dates, pitted and chopped
4 1/2 cups all-purpose flour
1 tbsp. ground cinnamon
2 tsps. ground ginger
1 1/2 tsps. baking powder
1 tsp. ground cloves
1/2 tsp. ground cardamom
1/2 tsp. salt
2 eggs
1 cup brown sugar
1 cup honey
1/4 cup blackstrap molasses
1 tbsp. water
2 tsps.
2 tsps. grated orange zest
1 tsp. grated lemon zest
3/4 cup confectioners' sugar
2 tbsps. whole milk
1 tsp. lemon zest

Directions:

1. Cover almonds with boiling water in a bowl.
2. Let stand for 1 to 2 minutes and drain.
3. Rinse with cold water and drain again. Pat almonds dry and remove skin. Allow almonds to dry on paper towels.
4. Place half the almonds in a food processor.
5. Pulse until finely chopped.
6. Add apricots and dates; pulse until fruit is chopped.
7. Reserve remaining 1 cup almonds.

8. Combine flour, cinnamon, ginger, baking powder, cloves, cardamom, and salt in bowl. Beat eggs, brown sugar, honey, molasses, water, almond extract, orange zest, and 1 tsp. lemon zest in a large bowl with an electric mixer until smooth. Add apricot mixture, blending until evenly distributed. Gradually stir in flour mixture on medium speed until dough comes together. Cover dough with plastic wrap and refrigerate for 8 hours to overnight.
9. Preheat oven to 350 degrees F (175 degrees C).
10. Turn dough onto a lightly floured surface and roll out to about 1/2-inch thick. Cut out cookies with a 2 1/2 to 3-inch diameter cookie cutter. Arrange cookies about 1 inch apart on ungreased baking sheets.
11. Lightly press 3 almonds into each cookie with tips towards the center to create a star pattern.
12. Bake in preheated oven until cookies begin to brown, about 12 minutes. Cool in the pans for 10 minutes before removing to cool on a wire rack.
13. Meanwhile, whisk confectioners' sugar, milk, and 1 tsp. lemon zest in a bowl until glaze is smooth.
14. Brush warm cookies with glaze and allow cookies to cool completely.

Christmas German Honey Cookies

Ingredients:

1 cup white sugar
1 cup shortening
1 cup honey
2 eggs 1 tsp. vanilla extract
1 tsp. baking soda
4 cups all-purpose flour
1 tsp. ground ginger

Directions:

In a saucepan over low heat, melt together sugar, shortening and honey. Let cool.
Mix together eggs, vanilla, baking soda and ginger.
Gradually add to cooled honey mixture.
Slowly add 4 cups of flour to mixture. Stir until well blended.
Drop by teaspoonfuls onto cookie sheets about 2 inches apart.
Bake at 350 degrees F (180 degrees C) until golden, about 12-15 minutes.

Christmas Gingerbread Men Cookies

Ingredients:

3 cups flour
2 tsps. ground ginger
1 tsp. ground cinnamon
1 tsp. baking soda
1/4 tsp. ground nutmeg
1/4 tsp. salt
3/4 cup butter, softened
3/4 cup firmly packed brown sugar
1/2 cup molasses
1 egg
1 tsp. vanilla extract

Directions:

Mix flour, ginger, cinnamon, baking soda, nutmeg and salt in large bowl. Set aside.
Beat butter and brown sugar in large bowl with electric mixer on medium speed until light and fluffy.
Add molasses, egg and vanilla.
Mix well. Gradually beat in flour mixture on low speed until well mixed.
Press dough into a thick flat disk. Wrap in plastic wrap.
Refrigerate 4 hours or overnight.
Preheat oven to 350 degrees F.
Roll out dough to 1/4-inch thickness on lightly floured work surface.
Cut into gingerbread men shapes with 5-inch cookie cutter. Place 1 inch apart on ungreased baking sheets.
Bake 8 to 10 minutes or until edges of cookies are set and just begin to brown. Cool on baking sheets 1 to 2 minutes.
Remove to wire racks.
Cool completely.
Decorate cooled cookies as desired.

About the Author

Laura Sommers is the Zombie Prepper Mom!

Helping you prepare for the Zombie Apocalypse! She is the #1 Best Selling Author of the "Recipes for the Zombie Apocalypse" cookbook series as well as over 40 other recipe books.

She is a loving wife and mother who lives on a small farm in Baltimore County, Maryland and has a passion for all things domestic especially when it comes to saving money. She has a profitable eBay business and is a couponing addict. Follow her tips and tricks to learn how to make delicious meals on a budget, save money or to learn the latest life hack!

Visit her Amazon Author Page to see her latest books:

amazon.com/author/laurasommers

Visit her blog for more life hacks or money saving ideas:

http://zombiepreppermom.blogspot.com/

Visit her on Facebook for up to date notices on what the Zombie Prepper Mom has cooking!

https://www.facebook.com/zombiepreppermom

Follow the Zombie Prepper Mom on Twitter:

www.Twitter.com/zombieprepmom

Other books by Laura Sommers

- Easy to Make Party Dip Recipes: Chips and Dips and Salsa and Whips!
- Super Slimming Vegan Soup Recipes!
- Popcorn Lovers Recipe Book
- Inexpensive Low Carb Recipes
- Recipes for the Zombie Apocalypse: Cooking Meals with Shelf Stable Foods
- Best Traditional Irish Recipes for St. Patrick's Day
- Awesome Sugar Free Diabetic Pie Recipes

May all of your meals be a banquet
with good friends and good food.

Made in the USA
Las Vegas, NV
21 June 2024

91325693R00039